WAKE UP!
TO ALL YOU ARE

WORDS AND PICTURES BY WINIFRED RICH

Copyright © 2012 Winnie Rich

All rights reserved. No part of this book may be used or reproduced by any means, graphic, electronic, or mechanical, including photocopying, recording, taping or by any information storage retrieval system without the written permission of the publisher except in the case of brief quotations embodied in critical articles and reviews.

Balboa Press books may be ordered through booksellers or by contacting:

Balboa Press
A Division of Hay House
1663 Liberty Drive
Bloomington, IN 47403
www.balboapress.com
1-(877) 407-4847

Because of the dynamic nature of the Internet, any web addresses or links contained in this book may have changed since publication and may no longer be valid. The views expressed in this work are solely those of the author and do not necessarily reflect the views of the publisher, and the publisher hereby disclaims any responsibility for them.

Any people depicted in stock imagery provided by Thinkstock are models, and such images are being used for illustrative purposes only.
Certain stock imagery © Thinkstock.

ISBN: 978-1-4525-4145-7 (e)
ISBN: 978-1-4525-3460-2 (sc)

Library of Congress Control Number: 2011907058

Printed in the United States of America

Balboa Press rev. date: 08/14/2012

For You Who Light the World.

For every child everywhere,
Love all that you can see;

Wake up to all you are, so
You can be all you can be.

With Love, Aunt Winnie

Thank you.

Amelia Albert is the delightful child in the pictures.
Amelia, you made this book all it could be.
I thank you.

To the special people, particularly Shannon Ernst
and Jill Harris, who helped and supported
me in writing this book,
I thank you and love you.

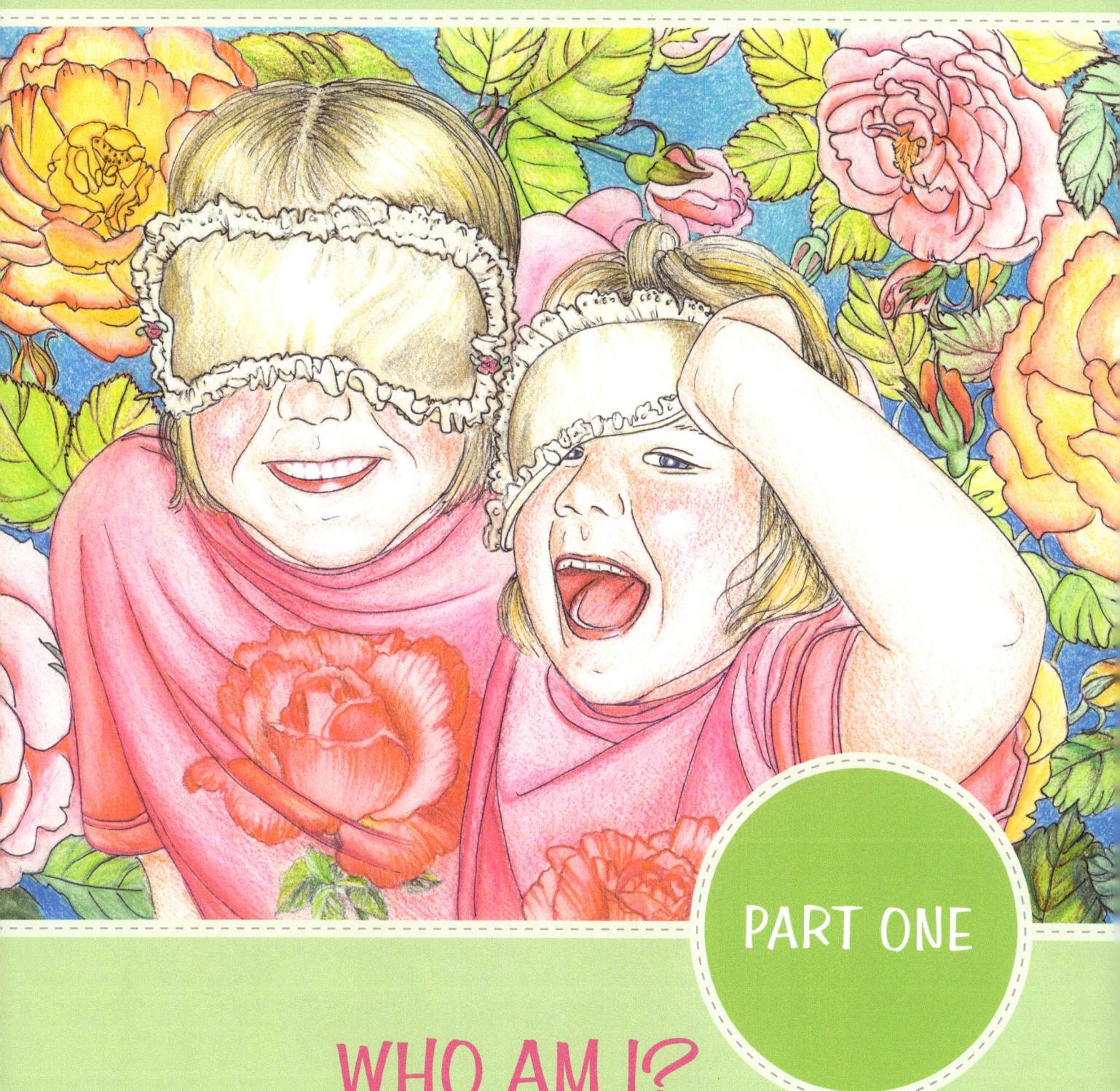

PART ONE

WHO AM I?

Wake Up! Discover that who you are is much more than a little body. You are as big as the Universe and just as amazing!

How? Let's find out!

Gigi wonders, "Who am I?
And why was I born me?

Who lives inside the rabbit?
Who's born across the sea?"

Who lives inside of me, and
Who looks out of my eyes?

Who IS that who is thinking?
Who laughs and loves and cries?"

"I look down at my body
And think that this is 'me',

But part of me I CAN'T see
Is such a mystery!"

Then Gigi hears God answer,
"YOU ARE A PART OF ME,

My Spirit lives inside you,
And gives you 'Life', you see."

Without that 'Life' you couldn't BE,
You couldn't DO a thing.

Just like a lifeless teddy
Or puppet on a string.

So, most of you is 'Spirit'
Not 'body', as you thought.

Your body is your 'earth suit'
That thinks you're in one spot!

What is our Spirit made of?
It's Love and energy,

All-knowing, light and beauty,
And all the joy you see;

Our Love is like the sunshine
That lights and warms and gives,

And you're a precious light ray
That blesses all that lives.

Because we share one Spirit
That sees through everyone,

See another as yourself
And know that you are ONE."

"You see, We are creation!
Each thing that's everywhere.

You see Us all around you,
Not knowing We are there.

We flow into each other
As parts of one big sea,

So YOU and all of NATURE
Make up the rest of ME."

"Look here, we're in the fishes,
In seas, and whales that dive,

That's US beneath the pebbles
In things that come alive!

The Earth is Love; WE are Love,
So, Love surrounds you, too.

Why, even blossoms Love you
As trees and rivers do.

Breathe in Love, and fill yourself
With worth and dignity

Then loving Life as equal
Will bring us harmony.

Your body is amazing!
Superb in every way.

So, give it rest, healthy food,
And exercise each day.

Thoughts you think and how you feel
Can hurt your body, too.

So, happy, healthy thinking
Will keep it well for you.

I made Life to be easy,
So have a lot of fun.

This makes your whole world better—
Your Joy has just begun.

I made everything from Love,
So you'd feel safe and fine;

Relax, let go, be happy—
And life will be divine.

The best thing you do in Life
Is just be happy, Dear,

For this lifts everybody
And everything that's here!

Love and laughter heal the world
So, YOU help change the earth!

Each person is important,
And priceless in his worth!

PART TWO

WHY AM I HERE?

You are here to *learn to love everyone and everything*. Why? Because I am in everyone and everything I made. I took my raw stuff and made mountains and stars, kangaroos, parsnips, and YOU. Our Love makes it possible for us all to live together happily in peace.

"Tell me, God, why am I here?
I loved my home with you".

You came to share your Spirit
In everything you do.

You came to live your Love, Dear,
Which melts away your fears.

This is how you grow your soul
And wipe away your tears.

Always listen to your heart,
Emotions are your guide.

Always choose what feels the best;
Do what feels right inside.

I can see what you cannot—
I'll tell you what to do;

Then let go – I'll do the rest
And show my Love for you.

First, Love all kinds of people—
For *they're all you,* you know;

How they believe and differ
Will always make you grow.

If you think folks don't love you,
You'll soon see that's not true,

Through loving and forgiveness
Their love will come to you.

Since everyone's your teacher,
Love who's in front of you.

Only see *your love for them*,
Not what *they think of you*.

Sometimes folks can yell at you,
When they're upset inside

Maybe, Dear, it isn't you;
So, Love should be your guide.

As well as all the people
Are creatures small and tall,

That share this planet with you,
And you can Love them all!

They think and feel like you do,
And need respect and care;

Your pets need all that you need
In homes that they can share.

Begin to learn from critters—
They'll teach you how to BE!

Watch their LOVE and GRATITUDE—
Their honest hearts are free.

Their courage, joy, and patience
Will surely show you how.

And they live in the moment,
So they trust and allow.

If you feel bad, LOVE someone—
Get help, and talk to Me.

Breathe and smile, think happy thoughts
Your feelings turn to glee.

Go out and play in Nature,
In trees and meadows fair,

How much better you can feel
When you have fun out there!

The Earth Loves you so dearly!
Let's make Her really clean,

Then She'll return to Paradise
All beautiful and green.

Her waters will be sparkling,
Her air so sweet and clear,

And gardens rich with ready food
Forever will appear.

Whenever you may need Me,
Be still—I'm in your heart

I'm in and all around you—
We cannot be apart!

We are a team—include Me
In all you try to do;

And allow me to unfold
My wondrous plans for you.

You need me, and I need you
To be my body there—

To hold your baby brother
And give him loving care.

You also help our wildlife—
They need our help these days,

But never interfere, Dear,
My ways are Nature's ways.

PART THREE

WAKE UP TO OUR MAGIC!

Your life comes to you by God's responses to your thoughts.
You make your whole world from your imagination!
What you think and feel now becomes your future.
I'll teach you how to make it HAPPY!

I made you in my image,
So you're Creators, too.

Make something out of nothing
From what's inside of you!

It's really very simple:
Imagine and believe;

Then your thoughts turn into things!
It's easy to achieve!

See what your dream will look like,
And *often see this view.*

Feeeel it's there. *Believe* it.
Know *you deserve* it, too.

Give thanks that it is coming,
Let go and *know* it's true.

So, ask for *good and glad* things
For *everyone* and you!

Bad things sometimes happen
That you don't understand.

They *come to teach you something*
So *you can make life grand.*

Sometimes bad things come from fears
Give them to Me—be wise;

Sometimes the way I fix them
Can be a fun surprise!

Suppose you've asked for something
That hasn't come to you,

Could it be the time's not right
To make your wish come true?

Feel what it's like to have it:
You're happy, safe, and free,

Feeling good gets rid of fear,
So you create like me.

You know that tears and anger
Won't bring what you desire;

So think of all the good things
That you want or require;

You are given what you want
Before you ask each day.

*You're always safe and cared for,
Remember that today.*

There is no death; don't worry,
It's just a change of clothes;

You let go of your "earth suit"
And take a peaceful doze.

Then, all at once you'll find that
Your Spirit's home! And then...

You begin to learn and grow
Until you live again—

Kids know what is important:
Do less while *Loving* more.

Lie back and watch the clouds change;
Hear waves upon the shore.

Be in Peace and live in Love,
Your body needs this, too,

Surround yourself with sunshine;
It's very good for you.

See Life here as the best place
To sing and dance and play;

When people work together,
It's Heaven every day.

We'll make the Earth so peaceful
From gratitude and glee

That everyone who lives here
Is warm and fed and free.

Because you make things better,
I am so proud of you!

You have a special purpose
That no one else can do.

Will you talk to animals?
Or make sick people well?

Just keep on dreaming, Sweetheart,
For only time will tell.

Each heart can hold so *much* Love!
Yet much more it can give.

This much kindness feeds a heart
So it can really live!

Put many hearts together
And see what they can do:

Why, anything, anywhere—
It starts with ME and YOU!

www.ingramcontent.com/pod-product-compliance
Lightning Source LLC
Chambersburg PA
CBHW060822090426
42738CB00002B/79